# Sun Showers

# &

# Moonflowers

# *Sun Showers*
# *&*
# *Moonflowers*

Raquel Medora

**SUN SHOWERS & MOONFLOWERS**



Printed in the United States of America.


*Cover art and illustrations by Raquel Medora*
*Photos on pages 112 & 147 by Gabriella Cortez*

ISBN: 979-8-218-88784-1

# Table of Contents

In loving memory of my dad and my papa.

**To the reader,**

This is a memoir of poems that began months before we found out the heartbreaking news of my dad's Glioblastoma diagnosis. It is written over a 10-year span of life filled with heartbreak, grief, loss, remembering, growth, and healing. The purpose of this book is to provide you with companionship on your journey with grief.

There is no right or wrong way to approach this book, just as there's no right or wrong way to approach your own grief. You can start from the beginning, middle, or the end. You can choose to color the pages, highlight words, write your own words, use glitter pens to add the shine and sparkle you want to see, but whatever you do, do it knowing you are not alone in this.

For additional context, I wrote quite a few of these poems my senior year of college in 2016, the year my dad passed away from brain cancer, and in 2017, the year my grandpa passed away. I cried every day and was sick several times that school year. I thought the grief and loneliness might consume me, but these poems helped keep me and the memories of my dad and papa alive. And so, I hope they help you too as there are rarely the "right" words in such a time, whether you've lost a loved one, lost part of yourself, moved on from friendships and/or lovers, moved to a new city, etc., know that grief is the pillow of space between love and time.

No matter where this book finds you in life, know that it was meant to. You are so exquisite, special, and brave for living every day with your heartache while gradually growing to hold more space for it.

Much Love,

Raquel

# Part I: Before The Diagnosis

*It's a dream. It's a dream. It has to be a dream.*

## Empathy

now I am sitting in a low-lying chair
under a kumquat tree in the early evening

I watch a bee pollinate flowers
dipping her head in deep,

nurturing the pink depths of each flower
petals falling down as she masters her way around

and it's hard to imagine
that behind this building and into the next

there is someone crying,
while the buzzing of this bee

and the motor vehicles at the street
are the only things bothering me

## November 2015

something's amiss / the wind
blows / my hair is standing
on end / not just leaves / or wind-chimes
sleepily singing or / sky slipping the first signs of winter
into the evening / palpitating, lingering /
calm / caressing
your hairs / light
the hallway
/ numbness / sleeping /
cancerous mutation /
darker than grey mornings / fingers
tickling up your spine / darkness resides
here now

## Greyscale

the world is black and white
and our minds live in between the lines

on a greyscale and sometimes
we are light and transparently checkered

other times we are dark – oh so dark –
you wouldn't know our checkered spots by name

amphibians swimming in the streams
flailing our arms and swinging our hips in circles

that fit into boxes
on a line between the light and the dark

on a sidewalk that is for sure white,
but black is the night

color only in our eyes
when we dream, looking through a window

into snippets of scenes
of perhaps the afterlife

a long story, incoherent,
and blurred feelings, the strongest of those

life is anything,
but black and white

## Falling for the Moon

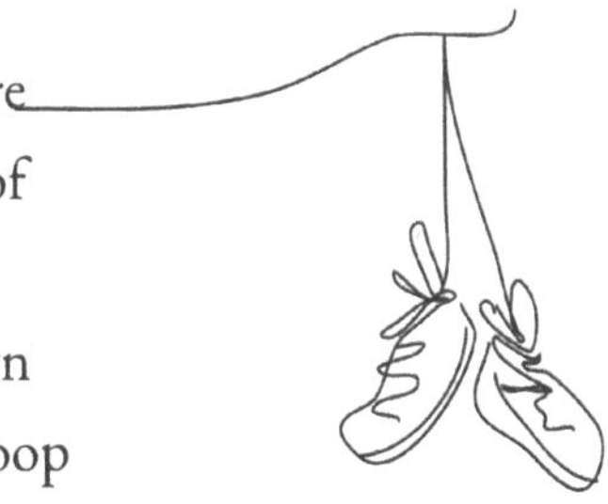

shoes dangle from the wire
a chair on the top of a roof

creaky stairs to creep down
underwear in a crooked loop

concrete cracking below
the earth's heart beats slow

downward spiral down
below earth's surface

into heaven's cradle
bees beneath the trees tickle

wings of birds above
a wondrous world to be caught in

who's to say it's not a dream?

# Part II: The Diagnosis

**Brain Surgery**

silence is broken
by a deep brazen moo

in the meadow
I trace my steps

back to an Easter
pink and golden eggs

as the sun sets
and the deer rest

unspoken words
on my plugged ears

## Doctor Stark

I see his face
and black hair,
his first name
escapes me –
reminds me
of the importance
of composure –
his posture stiff
and his teeth
too white,
like porcelain,
blue sleeves
unblemished
by his work.
Master of distance,
stiffness, distant
isle eyes, in a room
of one dozen crying
faces, eight hours
later, crick in the neck,
foreignness
I wish I could forget.

## Thoughts on Thoughts

Forgoing an inconceivable procedure under hyper-beams
and stringent lights glaring down lasers into a thick, tight
skull squeezing remnants of imagination and
bridge-building into oblivion.

These bridges kept breaking, destruction over construction
and cancer-causing agents intensified the rapidity in which
the spine collapsed on itself and you left us un-reconciled
and unrecognizable.

Glazed looks as thoughts pervaded the intercepting liquid
thoughts around an already emptying space where the soul
meets the mind and we kind of thought they were one and
the same, but now I know the soul and the personality
imperceptibly break at the destruction of the brain.

## My 21st Birthday

brainwaves sneak through intertwined threads
images of flashing colors – kaleidoscopically

take a microscope to the brain,
what do you see?

fuzzy pink matter –
scalp peeled back,

broken skull
brain barely functioning

pulling out pieces of tumor's claws
dreamlike-nebula

lacy light filtering impenetrable beams
neurons firing, thoughts transpiring,

personalities and dreams ensue
cut you open

sew you up again
try to twist a bottle cap

feel lame
home at last under moonlight

brave stars, hidden dreams, dreamcatcher moonlight
caught under a web's complicated simplicity

sit in the chair so long
your arms become the same color

a muted color
space out for hours

then come back to us
and explain your feelings again

call me on the phone
speak like we used to

realize you hadn't called at all
call me and forget all you had said

except to say,
*I'm so so sorry, Raquel*

## On Becoming Again, in Vain

I heard it in the night while I was trying to find myself and delay my anxiety. I tried to be quiet while I sang four of your favorite hymns. I tried to look for forgiveness. I tried to explain why I was seeking your love. I tried to open a doorway, but there was no handle or hinges or door for that matter. I tried to call you and failed; the phone disintegrated. I tried to listen, but heard no one for days. I tried to be patient but I bled fire in lieu of the rain. I tried to help you understand. I tried to let it sink in. I tried to tell you that you were going to die. I tried to deny that I was right. I tried to hug you, but you couldn't lift your arms. I tried to hold on to moments, but they kept passing away. I tried to disagree and then stopped trying. I tried to be strong. I tried to understand why people were staring at you. I tried to renew my faith, but I'm afraid god's had enough of me. I tried to find someone to protect me, but came to an opposite place. I tried to hold on to your hand, but all I could do was let go when my hand felt cold too.

## Painted Bunting

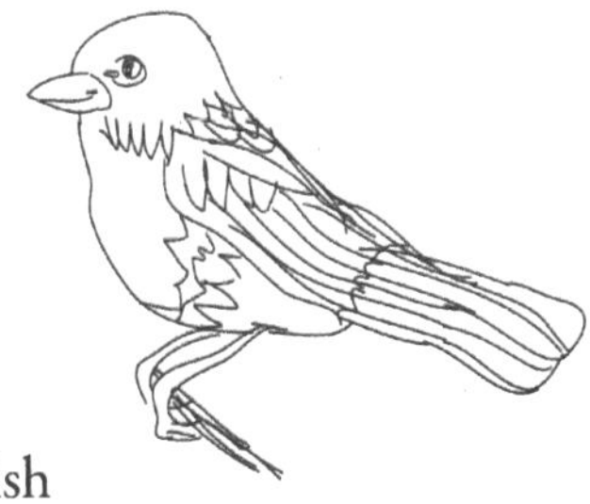

coffee you called "pixie dust"
sunday mornings

texts upon texts – enjambed gibberish
early enough to see the moon and the sun together

too early for me
one morning you shared

god's plan seen on a molecular level
at the dinner table over the creamiest, sweetest coffee

and the saltiest eggs – you couldn't quite taste
debating caused sunday morning seizures

everything caused morning, afternoon, night
shaky hand wrapped around the coffee handle

moon, hold tight, hold tight
no light in your eyes

glazed, flat-face mornings

summer mornings, birds color the sky

higher and – *god, they're in god's hands* –
can't talk anymore because you smell that morning

metallic, burnt oil smell –
steroids made your cheeks rounder

and somehow, your nose smaller
eggs on the floor

you pleaded for company in the mornings
you wanted us to drink pixie dust together

you wanted to tell me god's plans
when bright as the fresh day

a pair of painted buntings flew to the feeder
my world violently stopped

and my evening slipped into mourning

## September 1, 2016

life goes on, but I don't believe it to
I fell asleep

the metal letter R hanging from my bedroom door handle
*click, click, click*ed

back and forth, tapping gently
hushing a baby to sleep

until I fell asleep, a dream
came to me like syrup gently slipping

down my throat, soft yellows and pinks,
blues and oranges swirling beneath

my floating body as if lying on suds
my breathing steady, rocking side to side

in the swirls of life, not a care in the world,
just unimaginable peace and in the morning,

it was misty and grey and I felt I couldn't see
straight, the dream lingered with me, sleepy side-

effects as if to protect me
from the devastating call that would come

in the evening
later that day

# Part III: Loss

## The Month of Lavender

Steam rises off the rooftops
like fury flowing visibly from the temples.

Quiet nights ignite sleepless fire
inside while I try to decide my life, while

dried lavender loses its color
over time, then its smell,

and if you're not careful,
it turns a purple-grey.

From the floor I see the ceiling,
a purple-grey, and I wonder

what it'd be like if the world
were upside down.

The day is almost over
when I wake. Like never

existing. Blackness speckled
with light, staring off into space,

leaking anxiety onto every white page,
thinking about the breaths I take

and the ones I've given away.
In a wild blunder, I fall

asleep on the mahogany table.
Sometimes I have lavender

locked under my eyes,
undisguised.

## Can You Hear Me?

Deep belly-buzzing laughter,
full of life
radiating light through bright,
blue eyes and that big,
wide smile: delight,
unconditional love,
your love, my cornerstone of life.

My world is

b

r

o

k

e

n.

You're nothing.
Not even a *ghost* of a human.

Nothing.

Despair disappear.
Chills at 4am.
My imagination and yours have always been...overactive.
I think you are here with me...*but it can't be...*
sitting on the couch,
looking at me,
while I pass
through the hallway.

Passing... passing... passing...

## I remember

a time, one time
fleeing the feeling,
reality – falling fortunes
under moonlit lakes
dreaming here in the misty mornings,
we hold each other,
mental cats.

I seem to sound
like slurred moonlight
when there's snow
on the counter at 3
in the morning.

Tears fuel hostility.

I want answers and you say,

*but Raquel, people in hell want ice water.*

## Smiley-Faced Bandaids

I peel off the bandaid
every day
wax away the flakes of skin
in an agonizing pull
uprooting
but don't be fooled
I spent all day
ruminating
wondering if it would be
worth the pain
wishing for nostalgia
wishing I could lie in bed all day under the covers
or under ancient trees
in a cool grove with the breeze at my feet
a hum in my nose
pull the anxiety from her throne
share her zest with the bees
the bees deal with queens
they could help me
but I fear that wish has something over me
a worry that it still
won't make me happy

## I Want to Write a Happy Poem

I want to. But –
*g'night,* you say, *you'll be alright.*
Crying gains strength
in numbers.
Sweet dreams, Canary;
don't you know? You flutter
and chatter within the cage.
Moon songs.
Songs lusting after the stars
and their listless restlessness:
recipes for the hum of happiness.
So dance in the rain.
Sing under the moonlit rain.
Throw paint on the screen
and canvas. Sleep
and when you can't sleep, cry.
And when you can't cry, scream.
And when you can't scream, daydream.
Let it all out. Be loud.
Be alive.
Or just be,
sweet Canary.

**Sun Showers**

it's raining here now
a yellow rain
not gold, but yellow
a stale and staining rain

it stings the bottoms of our feet
with dampened dirt
and ash
you're ash

your shoulder beckons me
because I can't sit up straight

on my own

## Sitting

it's raining here now
but just beyond is an open piece of sky
bluer than god's eyes
sunrays fall onto the clouds

big whipped cream clouds

they look almost two-dimensional,
so this must be a dream

## Dreaming

it's raining here now
because I imagined it to
and I've been talking to myself again
and I miss you

and when I get up off these steps
to go inside
I imagine
two sets of wet prints
on the wooden deck
where we once sat
time after time
until time lapsed

and you existed
somewhere between the pellets of rain
yet to fall
and somewhere, somewhere
still alive in my brain

## Hole in the Wall

Avoiding the topic is like telling yourself you're not going to die. At the bar, it's easy to listen to wartime tales of Desert Storm and Kuwait, bad airport experiences, and Fourth of July stress. But by the close of the stories it's your time to talk, to open up just a crack, even if only a little. Inevitability strikes you down and in your drunken ebbs and flows, leaning to and fro, hanging from the edge of the wooden bar, you look over at the friend you came with, avoiding the guy you just met, and your heart and mind pour on until you mention *it*.

Their faces go grave.

## Moon to Sun as Autumn to Summer

The noisy faux chirping of insects from the other room juxtaposes the recent silence of cicadas and crickets in the yard. The sun sets in her usual way, but more noticeably now with darkness uttering her kind words before night. The usurper comes with her candles and crawling friends and she tells us of fiery chimneys and smoke to brave the night with silence. Nights, a reprieve from a long thickening day witnessing life via light set to fade, living life under the covers and shade, braving the closeness of the encroaching dark just the same.

## Wallow

withering into wilts
sun-tinged black

under my eyes, following
you out the door

heart beats stomach sick
sky turning from blue to grey

women walk along the boardwalk
the lights move along their face

hair shining black and gold
quietness overtakes our breaths

as we find our way home
a moment's notice is all it takes
the moments left to mourn

## Rivers Are Not Blue

I am blue. I am the blue sky. I am the blue boxers. I am the blue gravity, holy and unforgotten. I am the blue bruise, shades under your eyes. I am the blue tile, glossy and unclean. I am the blue river, bold and flowing under the veil of your skin. I am blue with envy. I am blue anxiety, curtain-crushing. I am bluebonnets, smothered by the photographed families. I am blue and I am what I am not.

**It's as if**

my tears
are a stream
t
r
i
c
k
l
i
n
g
down some
pre ------------------------ determined
path ,
although
the path
does feel a bit
haphazard
at times
it's as if the stream
meandered into the |||||||||||||| forest to become
a river ~~~~~~~~

until once
more the edges
of rocks
are softened
and the water ....................... thinned

to     become     a     creek

jagged     bed                    but dry

the pawprint–
trails
lining the
edges 🐾
imprinting some memories
of survival
along the
{{{{{{{{blades}}}}}}}}
of water
until
at long last
the stream opens     again
it is a river

when the river meets her ocean

she starts again

## It's Not Pretty to Cry

Wounded by the bay of my horizon, the tips of my toes on broken white shells, bleeding, yellow on the gravel of heartbeats. A throb, a sigh, weakness weakens the broken, falling through the cracks of the bridge, one slip and you lose everything. Shattered skull and brain matter scrambling to impart a fleeting thought to the escaping soul, that had ever-longed to flee its capture. The body lost feeling, memory, meaning. Even the cold hand invokes coldness in a warm one, as if beckoning to eternal sleep.

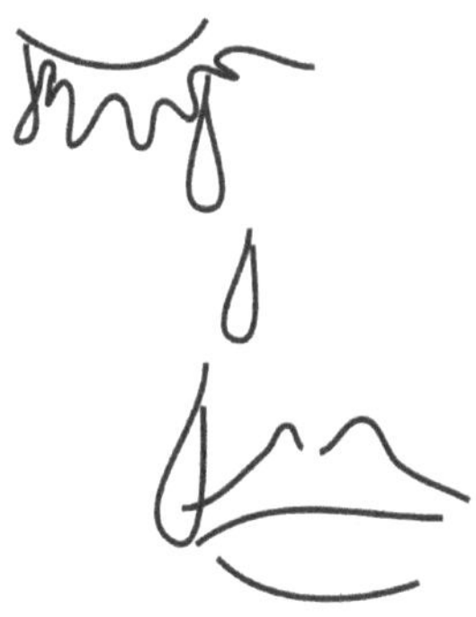

## My Gushing Geyser of Tears

floating on the back of a train, dozing
through tunnels, completely insane,

falling off the tree limb, berry splat,
stench rises beneath me, sweltering sun

simmers my insides,
spilling out onto the tongues of ants,

and aunts who squash me with big, ugly
feet, my, my, my big bluebonnet sky

streams of morning glory spilling
out long white pillows for ants,

hosed with old nuisance neighbors
crawling by their own accord,

and I ask for your help, your embrace,
the tunnel echoes my words back to me, flat,
on my wind-blown face

## The six-month mark

is nearing. Lug-nut slug. I'm squeamish.
Shattered night sky
like the dark ink
spilling out of my heart
onto the paper.
Twilight. Our torrent
nights. Half-hated.
Seize belief. Dreamlike.
Un-notable. Hazy
belligerence.
Circle on the ceiling-sky
glimmer flicker glow.
My skin
melting from my face.

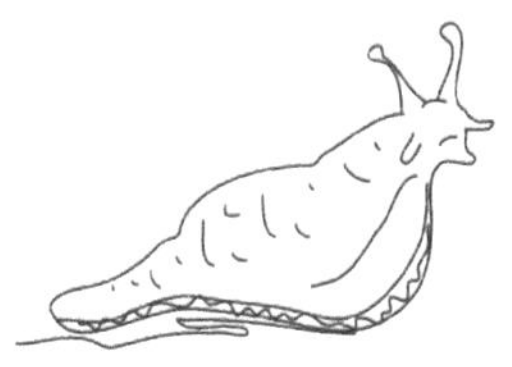

## Dense Hands and Headstands

blinded by some hopes and dreams
calling home those early evenings
dreading the in-between's: *hello-goodbye*
every time I would cry just to see your face, to be held
in your hugs, talk,
most of all is to talk,
and this song, that saying,

lightning fast life's not to last,
a quarter in the gumball machine
rolling round and round

not much longer than the flavor lasts

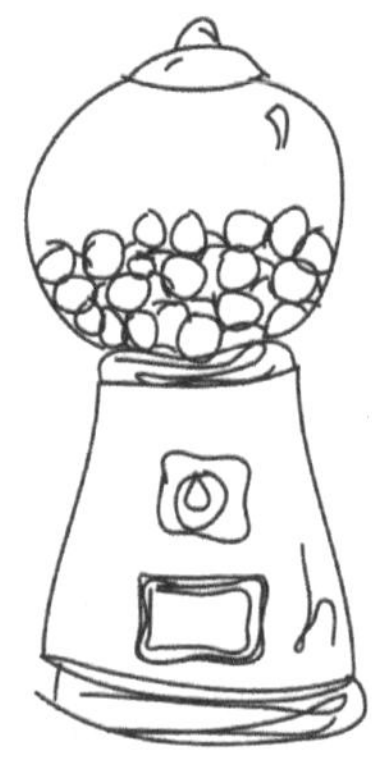

## I Didn't Get to Grieve You

*to my papa*

I miss
when cloudy days were warm

and I jumped over tiny train tracks
over racetrack-electric cars and into blades of grass

back in the back
*the good ol' days*

were made up of you
and grandma in the kitchen

while silent thoughts buzzed
over crossword puzzles

and I'd claim that the psychiatrist was in
evaluating, flipping through merck and devising

a medical treatment plan
because the botflies lived inside your skin,

*addicted to chocolate*, as you said,
once we made the steam engine steam

and I adored it
once I pretended to be a pilot

and flew planes on flight simulator
and drove cars around tracks

and in real life
at aunt nanalee's

where I first learned to drive
in the baby-blue, midsized suv

life was magic
it will never be the same

and it's not meant to be
meaningful conversations

fade into the distance
don't forget to tell me

what it's like
on the other side of the daisies

## 2002

We were driving down the Interstate in Ol' Betsy. Her light brown, fuzzy seats a reminder of a soft, familiar feeling. The sun glimmering forest green on the hood and bouncing back into the sky. Passing rolling hills and rocky cliffs jutting out as if to warn me – warn me of life's harshest days and its sublime beauty, of deserted and dried tears left on a broken-hearted face. Classic rock playing, the speakers booming and our voices belting out, mine against the restraint of the scratchy seatbelt under my chin, damp from my anxiety. My feet kicking under the seat, the windows cracked, letting the fresh forest air and red dust enter my daydreams. In the rearview mirror you look up to see me, your eyes squint around the corners and I know, you're still smiling at me.

**Granddaddy's Snores**

Everyone knows a good snore when they hear one.
We don't need to hear one to hear one.

It's that deep, throaty gurgle of familiarity.
That throaty gurgle that disrupts the thin air.

Sound waves almost tangible. Quiet interrupted.
A Saturday afternoon. The tv low with a game replaying.

Roast in the cooker aromatically filling the air. Matriarch
outside raking orange and yellow leaves.

A child reading in the kitchen.
Then he's breathing slower, steadier, noisier.

Suddenly a snore escapes followed by a short, close-mouthed
silence. And then another rupture of noise.

The cacophony continues, but not forever.
Absence is a place and a feeling.

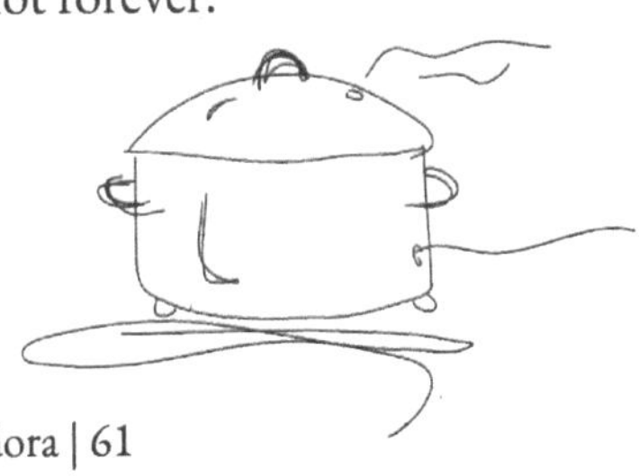

## Crying

When lightning strikes and sparks fly and its tingly and painful around the rims of your nostrils, a jolt of rock moves up your throat, and you can't swallow and you can't yet cry and it's painfully stuck like choking on the words you don't know how to say.

Perhaps it's goodbye, it so usually is, or unusually yet, the seeds of love denied trickling down the cheeks. Crying quietly or violently, choking on crying, crying after phone calls that remind you of someone you lost – when you see their smile so clearly, light dancing in their eyes, their words singing over space and time, and the tears come like stones ejected from your eyes.

You'd think the heart would feel relieved of the burden of these boulders and pebbles, but she swells with yearning, as if inhaling for a big, deep sigh. The tears subside and emptiness takes her place. Your heart slowly deflates with or without the jagged stabs from sinking boulders falling to the silty bottom of the lapless lake, sometimes though, the jabs in the heart remain and you decide it's time to finish typing that email – clacking keys – as if the crying never came.

**Grave**

Groceries on a Sunday – gotta pick up cabbage and sausage, turning each head in my hands to touch, analyze – but that's a vision, that's a polaroid photo in my brain that I'm reminded of in the wine aisle at 9 o'clock on a Sunday – remind me to pick up a case for the classics – but I've lost a lot of sleep since then. I'm stuck in aisle 5 or 6, whichever one got you sick and on the 1st day of September, a Thursday after 5, you drew your last breath, my last breath of hearing your memories, your trauma-stories nibbled down into the reptilian brain, perhaps knee-deep in onions and soups and corn on the cobs. I would never spend enough time with you. I could wander the oversized aisles for hours, even under those fluorescent lights, just to be close to you, just to speak with you, just to hear your laugh once more, idioms and Brad-isms. This world is not the same. It lacks luster without you.

## Ashes in the Sky

a little blonde bird lives in my mind
he lulls and harks in the dark

when I see the clouds rolling, curling, and folding
in the vastness of the bright, baby-blue sky,

the sweltering sun comes down on my back,
soil stings the beds under my nails,

buried deep into the roots of my skin,
digging up a periwinkle bed,

the breeze shimmies through the branches,
a deep voice calls out, vibrating waves

and I am caught in between my molting skin
and the changing colors between the lines in the leaves,

an iridescent shine like an incandescent, dusk sky
letting go of a palm-full of sandy-grey ash

releasing you back to the sky
only to find

that you still sparkle in the light

## My Tingling Ajna

I keep rubbing my forehead,
frantically, trying to subdue the itch
the nervousness
rushing to a single point
shushing my clogged memories
leaving pimples across my forehead

the skin remembering the kiss
from my father's lips
dotingly, approving

my muscles tense
from frowning at people
tinged with the grip
from the ambivalent moon
like my crescent nail
pressed against my loosening skin
and my nerves that keep tickling me
timelessly, sensing the lost, incessant buzzing

rubbing like sliding a pocket door open
to take a peek and see who's been waiting

knocking impatiently
trying to say hello to me
behind this psychic eye,
itching to be heard
and seen

**Let Go**

the noose is locked around my neck
after signing a waiver

saying that I wouldn't cry
if you died

and still the longing in my lungs rests,
the holding on so hollow,

to every bitter last breath
do the embers of soul

scatter like thoughts in the brain
or is it tethered by stars

unable to let go
with the rain?

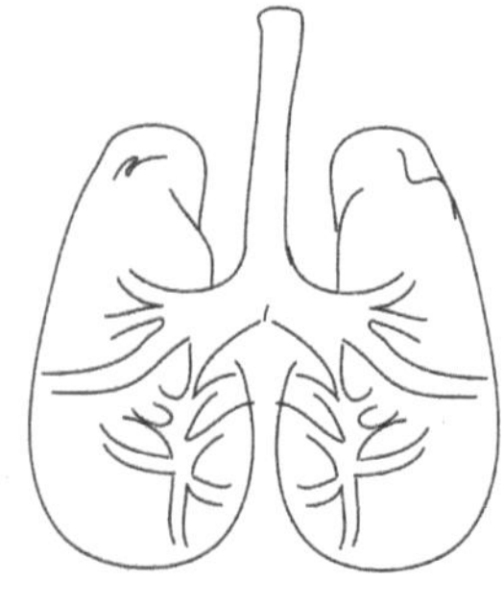

## Enough

They tell me to have faith as if it's as easy as breathing.

They say to close my eyes and envision love, protection, and peace.

They say it's as easy as one, two, three.

But for those of us who have lost everything, or only one thing dear, try telling them to trust.

Tell them to trust what now causes them pain.

Tell them how their pain is all the same, or worse, tell them how their pain could never compare to yours.

No. I will not. I cannot.

My pain belongs here.

Let it rightfully take up space.

It belongs in the grass, in the red oak leaves, and off the tips of the wings of flying zebra swallowtails.

It belongs in the morning sun, rising to remind us that the pain may stay, until one day, eventually, it transforms into something much more complex and obscure: love.

Love elates, shakes the happenstance of the everyday. It's the cushion to embrace when times are shrouded in grey. And when that love is lost once more, the cycle of rain begins again.

# Part IV: Life Without Dad

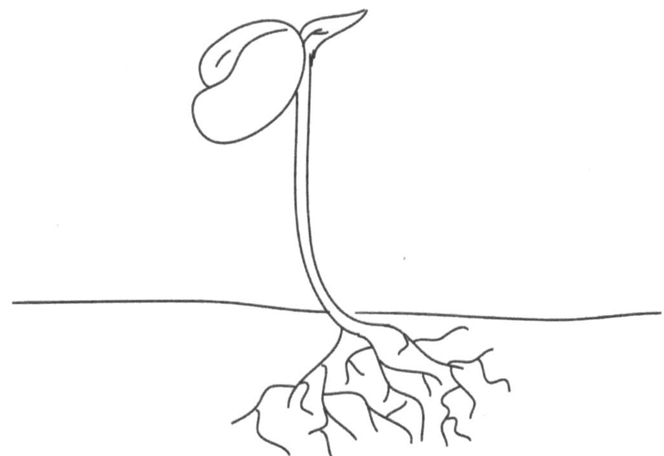

## "Quit Your Complaining"

I think that's a load of shit
sorry my perfectionism made me a tyrant

sorry I'm still saying sorry
like bronchitis lingering in my lungs

I've never seen a can of worms,
have you?

worms everywhere
every year I find myself digging up a new garden

digging up old generational weeds
the old I can't seem to heal from

wounds and tea
they pair so nicely

when you cut an earthworm in two
it regrows its back-end immediately

why can't I do that?

it's all shit you know

every bit, every plant, every fruit from every tree
shit everywhere

I tell myself it doesn't matter who picks me
as long as I pick me

sometimes that makes me feel better
and sometimes that makes me want to scream

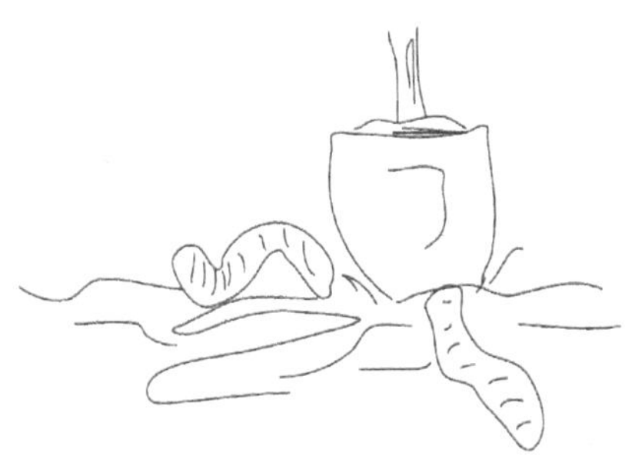

## Is this the violence you dreamed of?

clipping the thin neck of a premature rose bud
spilling its life expectancy all over its green, leafy feet

hooking a worm that wriggles violently
with each prick thereafter
flung into the water
what's left of its dismembered body
floating to the floor
lost like missing children

is this the violence you dreamed of?

bodies in piles,
bodies in graves,
bodies dismembered

I won't close my eyes
no, I won't close my eyes
they need to cry
don't close your eyes

### I Dream of Whales

the dream dictionary says
whales are intuition and emotion
I swim with whales
and I'm not afraid
I walk the border around their cage
I go to an aquarium and see their eyes
turned toward me
I swim with whales
I go on a whale watching trip
but the whale I see is a tire
I get in the ocean
hoping to swim with the whales
I see a turtle
she stares at me
when I swim closer
I see her eyes do not move
she is filled with plastic

*Emotions are like a garden. Go in, nurture them, take what you need, and leave when you're ready.*

**Sadness**

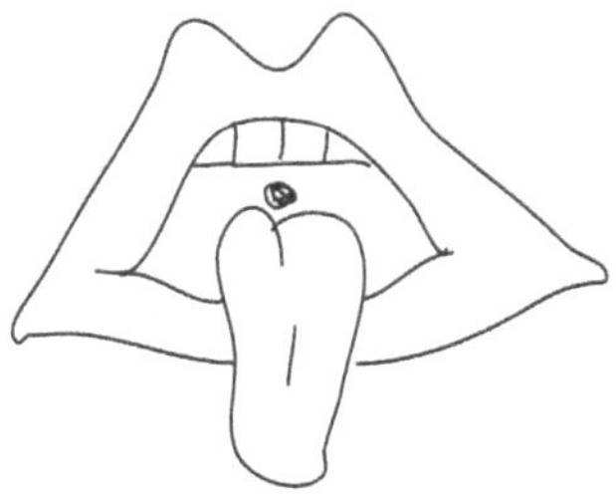

sits quiet on the tip of my tongue
aloof, jarring, stiff with potential
and power like no one

sadness sits quiet
hooded in the cavern
she's motionless, trapped
and seizing my tongue

will she slither into anger?
or hold my tongue?

will she bite the fears
so that the tears may come?

will she undress
sharing her messy attraction?

sadness sits quiet on the tip of my tongue
motionless, waiting for me to name her:

I'm missing someone

## Criss-Cross Crows and Goats

Can you turn a flower into stone?
Even a rose with her thorny legs, juicy insides,
even a rose upside down on the wall, papery and dry?

No, even she will not grow so cold and heartless and lifeless.
No, even in her death, she is delicate, sharp, fine.

A cold, grey stone is what you ask her to be, to prevent
bending, breaking,
bleeding, losing leaves,
but what of the fox, the coward, the goat?
What of the moonlit webs,
the wolf cries, the cross crows?

She tries and tries and tries.

Her color will not mute, her stem firm in its root, the
sharpness more apt than stone's jagged edges to dilute the
inadequacies of apathy.

Perhaps, instead, the world must transmute.

## Coriander Moonlight

chills from languid past
côte de rhone
the holidays falling through glass cracks
in the rat-trap-gutters
bare feet
the shimmering and buzzing
wheezing of life in the sky
who wouldn't want to be a dragonfly?
we could fuck while we fly
in the water above champagne glass
in flutes along the sea drinking fruits we cannot see
we see the orange glow
the pale yellow sky
coriander moonlight
no silence here
no peace
we cannot hold on to anything
except our bodies
but even our breath will decay
the clouds will become summer moons
and our mouths will open to dirt and ash and everything
devilish from the past

godless nation, unconsummated
I am on the traceless steps of your tongue and here I am
but for your grace
your goodness
your delight
fallen from the fucking sky
hold me and tell me everything will be alright

## I sat with fear

and she told me her secrets. She said that when she was young, she held open her hand, and there lay a fly. The fly turned to larva. The larva burst into a million pieces to feed a million baby birds' mouths. She looked at me and said that I am a larva. I wondered how many times she would cut my face before I'd stop feeling pain. I replied that I wish I had been born a bee.

## It's Raining in Austin Today

as if the sky knew
how to empty our pain

reflecting the faces of women whom have known
nothing of safety and security

of pure rain
rain from collections of eyes to douse the collective pain

the fire that's been burning into the night
the midnight mornings

losing, losing, losing,
the rights to empty the baskets we are obligated to carry

## There is No Precipitation Without Evaporation

no darkness without light
no soil without your ashes
composted, eventually
as the scraps of friends' and families' memories
become the pieces of you
you leave behind
you *left* behind
the wake of you
mocking what it means to be awake
and sometimes, something like an orange hammer
or swans on a lake
or seeing pixie dust
or hearing a song that comes on in synchronicity with life
takes the word "present"
and morphs it into something else,
wildly different than what it was

**September 2019**

Bat-shit crazy on a Tuesday with knee-high socks, hot pink hair, and platinum blonde underwear – I can't get that Texas sweet tea out of my tastebuds or that espresso-gluten-free-mousse-cake or that Irish coffee. I can't seem to find you. I've looked *everywhere*, but I haven't stopped bleeding. All I have is a tape measure to put between my teeth that keep chipping away just like earth and how we decay. Can you call me? It's been three years and some-odd-days and I can't find you. I know it's here, that red lipstick I wore when I was ten to pretend to be the person I am today, but fuck today. Today is for reminding me how gratefulness is unattainable and that everything in grasp is clearly gone, wisping away between the sails. Fucking drain this clogged memory and maybe unbend the edges of this time warp that we are enduring. Do you taste the spray of the blue ocean's blood? Have you ever looked at the repetitive waves and realized it's not the lightening that's angry, but the ocean and her bending? They thrash and brutally brush us from mouth to bay. I lick my lips of that salt as sand rubs my eyes grittily. When there is a hole in a heart like mine, I become the waves, salt, and ocean spraying, striking, violently, *violently*.

But I take the dandelions between my teeth and bite until all the little parachuting pappuses float away. Cream cheese on a bagel, I should have, I would have, if I could have done it all differently.

**My Friend,**

There are no words that make this better. But I can tell you that you're not alone. I can say that you are good enough, and loved, and the feelings of relief you feel because you no longer need to fear losing her, are normal and expected. Love is thick, intertwining, and tangled when the loss comes. It's no wonder we feel empty and guilty and afraid with a growing black hole in our stomachs needing to be filled by a connection, however tangled and barbed-wire-sharp it may be. That hole exists now, so remember your love for yourself, your love for trying. That dull aching, the dark trenches you must now wade, are unavoidable. Sometimes you fall and rest because there's nothing else you can do, and that's okay. There are no words but, I'm with you and I love you.

xoxo,

Raquel

*Always stop to ask the trees for guidance.*

## Roses and My Rage Garden

My how these feelings have grown so big
look up and see their giant green leaves
spread out, providing shade.

*What a sturdy stalk.*
I say, patting the chunky green thing.

*What's it made of?*
you ask, looking up, admiring the great green beauty.

I say,
*Oh a mix; just a little rage, determination, fear,*
*disappointment, disgust, shock, hatred, annoyance, and I*
*watered her with the words spun from the hate and injustices*
*of the world. Look at how she grows.*

*I'm impressed. You must have a green thumb,*
you say as if this garden didn't grow on its own.

I pluck a rose, I say,
*It's for good luck. Our love must rebel.*

You pin the symbol to your shirt like a teary hug. You thank me and say,
*Tomorrow, same time, find me in my garden; you'll love the way the shrouded trees have grown, no longer ashamed of their thick roots and touching leaves.*

I smile, wave,
*Tomorrow indeed.*

**Pick Apart a Prayer**

as I pick apart a leaf
breaking it into uneven halves

then quarters and examining
the veiny, internal threads

the root, like a vessel, umbilically
connected and combined

until I ruin it, shred it, throw its jagged
pieces beneath me

an end of an end,
generously broken
by grace

## Pull Out my Heart, Violently

crimson blood
crisp to the touch,
dries in the heat
on the orange rug of dirt
under hell's setting sun
wailing into the night

unsteady vibrations
upending and I want to smooth
the coarse coat
of a lined zebra's shoulder

instead I cry silks
and unfinished crystal threading bones
crisp mornings from the dusty night
brighten the light within
until dusk and crimson
meet white tusks of sunlight
rise to meet me
in the awakened day

**Death on my Doorstep**

baby bird curled up
tiny feathers still forming
I spin it into symbolism
and think of an old part of me
that has died

there is no room for her anymore
to wallow and take up space
that mouth is too much to feed

or is it a symbol of friendships
one that came to an abrupt end

when I see its limp body
with flies tricking my eyes
telling me that there is still life inside
I must leave, unlock the door
wash my hands immediately

the image of death still lingering in my brain
as if it had touched me

## Chakra

sipping on crystals
golden rains in a small yard
believe with your heart

if emptiness is all you desire
drive the desert away
awaken your heart with fire

rekindling connectivity
electricity and sleep

I won't be your unbroken burden
I  carry load-bearing walls
I cradle and cuddle and hold hope up high

you are my highest regard
thoughts dripping with perception

relative realities
flames laughing in the night

swirling sage and handing out marked cards

keep the coat
you'll need it for all your rain

## Years Later

napping and not waking
what if, what if
what if he put a cap in his mouth
took apart a toy
choked
while the door was closed
what if he doesn't wake
what if the sun does not rise
and the moonflowers never die
but us, but us
we are the moon reincarnated
and where do we go
from here
from here
where you left me
left me alone
the most alone
without a mother
without a brother
with a dying grandfather
and a grieving grandmother
and friends that likely wouldn't be my friends

years later
what happens then
but the sun rose
day after day
as if it could not grieve
the losses
countless losses
over and over again
every day
but you weren't just a loss
you were a devastating tsunami
tidal waves of tears and wails
and awakenings
because the destruction
left me in its wake
and I refused to release
and let go
of hope
that the sun rising
would improve my state of being
would bring the joys
I could not embrace
while lying, half-alive

at the bottom of my darkest cave
and what if I must return
what if
what if
my life is a series
of griefs, great and small
what then would it mean
to be alive
half a person still
lost and filled with growing loss
but they tell me
this is not true
I will wake and find happiness
it'll look different than before
this isn't a glitch
that would be an insult
to our creator
to think
your death and the timing
was by accident

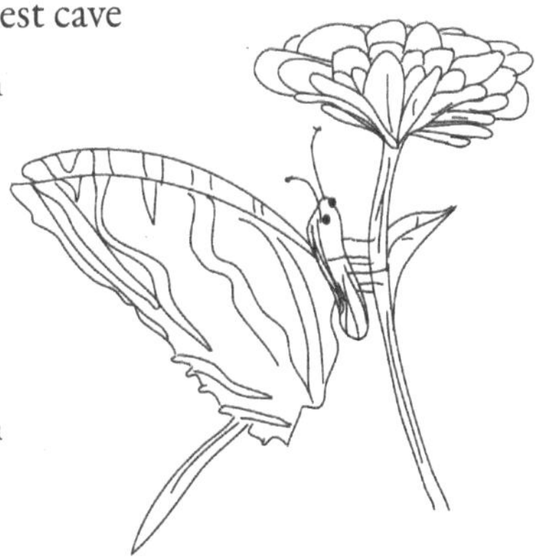

**Misconstrued**

constructed by a six-letter name
I am riveting
selflessness
antiquated customs
I am harboring
burdens
scribbled traumas
I am speaking
sweetness
muted symphonies
I am drifting
flowing
liquidated unknowns
dream of me and I am there
dream of me
dream of me
dream of me

**Can you taste my sadness?**

forlorn and longing
I'm not yet gone
but feel time
closing in on me

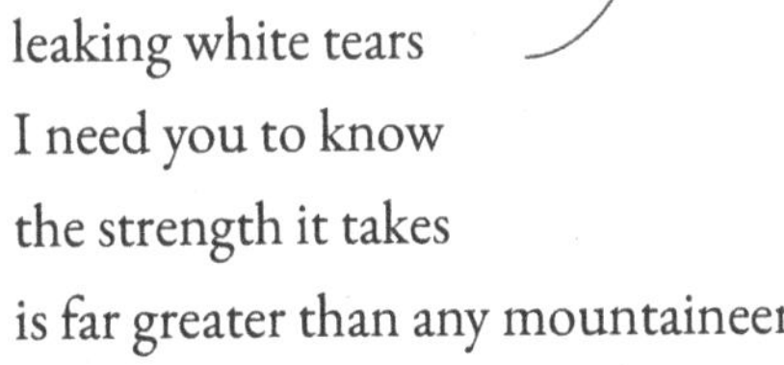

leaking white tears
I need you to know
the strength it takes
is far greater than any mountaineer

I cry thinking of the hours
we will spend apart
my heart aches
when you look at me

as I walk out the door
I must remember
love lasts longer
than these last moments
apart

## Ipomoea Alba

evening pours over the yard
the moon illuminates your unfolding petals

fireflies blink and glide
perhaps too delicately

for the windows glow inside through the cracks in the blinds
the house is quiet except for crickets, toads, and cicadas

they vibrate and echo
as if to welcome the dead

to walk softly by them on this night
it's late summer

the flowers spread and bloom a stunned stomach
filling with expanding darkness

emptiness,
the memories evaporate

clutching, anything

distancing from what one thought was real

real as this night
real as the poison

leeching, spilling, bleeding beautiful pain
slinking outside

to stand over the blooming moonflower
devoid of feeling

floating
moonflower, beacon in the night

sweeping vines
gripping the edges of the earth

toward our naked feet
blank and waiting

for the clipping
of someone's opening hands

white and moving toward moonlight
bringing with it

the remnants of love
lost to time

## Everything is Backwards

by everything I mean
iotas I mean
atoms I mean
atomic f-
bombs and caricatures
from christmas parties
what I mean
is I'm calling
and ringing in my ears
from the year 2002
same numbers
same year before —
I think what I mean
is when I look at trees:
red oaks and live oaks
and sycamore cypresses
I see a seed and hear the
sappy words you were
telling me
like *forever is forgotten*
and *what's lost is gone forever*
I mean

to put down the phone
but on a receiver
and I keep on
keeping calling me
I bought an iota
of time
slime slipping between cracks
between my fingers
like twirling the chord
while listening to breathing
an *I love you*
an unopened can of cancer
toothache, root canal
nasal spray, ash tray
disinfected, oil-guzzled
lobster tails or shrimp
or fake colored candies
what killed you, exactly?

*You may feel stuck now, but you are powerful and can overcome the fear you perceive.*

## Lost Bulbous Gumdrop

I'm frantic. Absolutely insane. I can't remember the last time a tear drop fell from my face.

*It's ok to go ahead and be afraid, take shelter in the change that's taking place.*

Chaos. Utter stage four tornadoes metastasized and blown away.

Trigger to the forehead, how impermeable are the untouchable thoughts we can't think once under the daisies?

Blame is not to bear on those who left us this way, but love and misunderstanding and bruising ourselves into believing that staying is far more valiant than leaving, which is a goddamn lie.

Love is everywhere, a merciless and destitute saint.

## Curmudgeon

Words on my lips, words on my lips, what words on my lips, in my throat, not like this, wish to be spoken? Red as lipstick. Reddened cheeks burn from the cold wind. Being in a body is uncomfortable. Walking the aisles, flipping my hair, back and forth, and back again, thinking one way more favorable than the other. Pinching my lip between my teeth. Mumbling of thinkings. Rubbing my cuticles. Rubbing my neck where there are now skin tags and moles like frays from the daily rubbing, physical thinking. How the thoughts pour out of me. Blemishing my skin walking away in words with the wind. Expressions on my face. Breaths under my pursed lips. Thoughts bundling up and walking this way then that. Thoughts caressing the lobby of this lot. Thoughts breaking out in bickering brevity, quick with depravity. Cycling thought patterns. A thought here for there. Outward and inward all depends on within. How the thoughts love my lips, and the vibrations of my tone going over and over their play a million and one different ways. Spilling out red everywhere reminding us where it is that we stay.

**I see red spots**

glaring at you
wiping a towel of sinister
disaster over
memories and holes
and unholy matrimony

trust like a sacred iota
an alibi of sand
glass fragments
shards of my hopes
funnel through this glass
liquifying this ball
of ice
an array of emotions like a viewmaster
tiptoeing around the inevitable
truth

words escaping
throwing buckets of throw-up buckets
orphaned and alone
the violent broken home
inside

targets for the darts
I keep throwing
keep  morphing
keep melting
keep wishing that some spellbound love poem
would bash me upside the heart
heal these feelings so precisely
feelings that are as quiet, illusive, and daunting
as the wind running its fingers through windchimes
belting out loud howls
serpent next to the sun
the sun and her anger
my how the mountain grows
but just such

the gospel of ants see me as quite unjust
creeping toward an inevitable end
wondering which foot comes next
and tripping on the trails
following trellises
up and around the stems
of grief

and her resurrections

## My Brain is Messy

Maybe I should clean before you come in, step inside my chaotic space, newspaper headlines tossed on the side chair, half-eaten bowls of instant noodles left to get dry and crispy like the half-eaten thoughts, hard to digest, especially all at once. There's too much to take in. I want to say it's like an art museum, hanging art in no particular rhythm or set font, hanging there for me to walk around and see what a lovely mess life can be, see whatever is left of the dirtied rugs. I say don't forget to wipe your feet, I want it clean, I want it neat, I want each thought to be compact, complete, I want to see the magic, the epiphanies, the beautiful connections all about me, right in front of me. In the dead of night my heart tinkers with the little lights, when the places inside my brain take shape, like neighborhoods, frequented getaways. I sense I've been here many times, a certain feeling, a feeling of certainty. I'm sorry it's so messy, it's just, I keep thinking, I can't stop thinking, you wouldn't believe the chatter in this room, the way it's splattered paint and unopened mail, and rocks, why are there so many rocks? Paths from so-and-so from the little restaurant we went to in the Vietnamese mart on rainy and cold Sundays and the trips to the store, the fluorescent lights, laughing together, and in connected thinking completing each other's thoughts, and over here a trip and a fall on that pebble-glued dock before my water bottle almost rolled into the abyss of the lake and the purple lightning struck the tree in front of me, branches burning and cracking into the inlet pond, and my seventh birthday and the gel pens and black paper, before my life began to rot from the outside to the inside to the outside once again, and what about the thought that the connectedness is as real as it is a memory, is happening now as it happened then but still yet the rest is unwritten or perhaps by now I know the control is within by letting go and what then?

**I'm told**

we are all one
from one source

from cosmic dust
rippling energy

yet when I dream
vividly of a place

people and their feelings
those in the dream

are just a reflection of me
like what I imagine

matrix theorists believe
is our reality

## Lights in the Darkness

the happiness
the feeling

at 3 I thought dreams were reality
and being awake was a dream

at 23 I thought my misery
deserved company

at 28 I couldn't understand
how to sit quietly

in systems complacently

humming to the computer buzzing
my head swimming with energy

intercepting something of a lost reality
so I laid in the grass

filled up to last my cup of longing
for an entire eternity

## Entrapped

It's not the cage
keeping me,
it's my own sense
of mortality,
the fear knotted
inside of me, clenching
too tightly,
but it's imagined,

there is no place
I need to leave
except the one
around my heart
keeping me.

## A Guide: How to Apologize to a Wasp for Killing its Family

I spent the weekend ruminating on my story
not quite reminiscing on the details

slipping into the tightly swaddled larvae's dreams
when I whacked the nest from the ceiling

the shovel was long and heavy
and my arms were weary

I shocked myself with my intensity
as if fire was already burning in my veins

displeased by their baby-making residence
in the hallways of my brain

in the corner of this camp, this porch
this under-lit and quiet banquet for lovers

to sleep and seep into their hives
I yelped and ran and felt the pain

not painful but hot
throbbing like a flu shot

in my arm
breathless and swatting

I leapt inside
heart pouncing and bouncing and tripping

over my curled up toes
and weeks later

a wasp snuck in through the door
whispered and buzzed

trying to escape
and intimidating us all the same

upon closer inspection
its darkness told

of the weaponless stinger
and it's funny how we worried just the same

because space is still a place
in need of protecting

# Part V: Letting Love In

## Winter's Love Poem

the wind through the leaves
the plants are secretly

alive, hiding their aliveness
in death to the visible eye

in their nakedness,
raw stems and branches

and the wind is unrelenting
and the frost burns

the leaves left over from fall
until the world is shaded

in grey and brown
then once again

green stems
emerge up from the ground singing,

breathing life into our hearts
for all is not yet lost

**I want to say sorry,**

but I know better than to let self-deprecation depreciate my value so intensely, so quickly.

I wanted to let my feelings dissipate, but they became something far greater; they let loose like running horses right out of the gate.

I wanted to believe in fate, I wanted to sit here and say I was fated to meet such wonderful souls, but I'm only one piece and sometimes I feel incomplete not knowing the feelings of others after deep interactions of feelings and thoughts pouring out of me.

I'm sorry if I wanted to go deep, if all I ever wanted was the deepest connection, deepest emotion, deepest feelings crossing back and forth so fast the two of us made beautiful electricity.

I allow the sorry, for I am sorry for holding these expectations so high it's no wonder my disappointment dropped me down from the sky, that the love of my life is still me, alone, searching, looking out the window to see myself looking back at me, my thoughts echoing in a chamber with me and only me to hold them and keep them company.

I tell myself it's ok to feel crazy. To feel crazy is the better half of my senses getting the best of me, the empathy in an apathetic world where only one half of the sexes know how to properly say sorry.

And sorry is how I feel for knowing how absolutely mind-boggling these deep human connections can be, the lasting effects for days, holding hands, searching in eyes, finding harmony in the most disharmonious times.

If I could draw you a self portrait of me I'd look the same but you would see the outpouring of love in the shape of tears puddling around me.

## It's Been a Bad Year for the Herbs

the pests suck and suck
each plant dry
dried of nutrients
dried of juice

I'm not sure how to stop them
I sprayed the white floating shits
with neem oil and vinegar
mixed with a bit of residual hate

they said that it'd take a few days
it's been weeks
marigold, rose of sharon, rosemary, sage,
they die and they die

names of women
who didn't make it to the second date
they shrivel up into curve-backed old ladies with canes
the color of alimony in wooden boxes

lowering into their graves
heathens crawl on my feet

bite my toes like I'm something sweet
the pain annoys me

I slap them off and pinch their sides
love won't stay even when it finds me

I try to save myself
with argan oil and rose quartz
inner peace tea and journaling
I go out and lie in the grass

3 vultures circle me
6 higher above
infinities
looping round and round

merry go round my anal brain
the sun echoes hope
but the clouds move slowly without purpose
ambling the curve of the sky

*a bubble* she says
*we're living in a bubble*

and I can't help but laugh
at the absurdly meaningless nature
of everything

## My Love is Not Guaranteed

war is ongoing in this world
and somehow

I'm more concerned with the war within me
the war between remembering and forgetting

the war between my heart
pulling on my stomach strings

the war between relief and pain
the war between fear and anger

it wants me
it all wants to consume me

but I keep looking in the mirror
and I know my truth

I know my bravery and beauty
my talents and heart

my intellect and most importantly

my soft love

which isn't always guaranteed
it comes in waves

sweeping, crashing
then slowly subsiding

gently gliding
across the tops of the sea

## Pain Relief

not a pill to relieve pain
but the state of being in two worlds

separated by the lowly, sick stomach
caught up in a whirlwind

of short-term love
and told that despite what was said

the future is unwanted
with me

shaking the jitters out of my bones
and sleeping on the street

I'm fondly aware
of my own state of being

held tightly
coiled around my daydreaming

they cannot keep me company

and although I saw it coming

I still feel it's shocking
I wanted more

need I say less
more time

more kisses
more conversations

more depth and vulnerability
I wanted you to be my safe haven

the home I call to when the weight
of the sad world burdened me

I wanted to tell you my secrets
and kiss you patiently goodnight

how shocking
you sped up

then pulled the e-brake
how can I forgive you

when I hate the beautiful orchid that's blooming again
and the loving notes signed *xoxo*

and your heart was so lovely to hold
and your words so soft to touch

and our hands and bodies placed in harmony
mirroring and loving

I'm sick
how I let love in

and let it break me

## Expiration Date

the jar of dill pickles
in my fridge

lasts longer than you
and lemons in the cooler

honey
apples

candied kisses
infested marigold leaves

drying sage and sunflowers
unopened letters on the counter

oil in my car
tar and toxic masculinity

because it is toxicity
healed only by the breaking of lines

on the invisible walls

trapped in the confines of your own making

the destiny you decided on
but sadly

you say you're cursed
and the only curse I see

is lying with you
and calling you into the creek

when you asked me
*what's that look, Raquel?*

I lied
because I was afraid

you'd say no to me
but honestly?

the look meant
I wanted to kiss you

badly, feverishly
roll in the water

play
laugh for days

co-create
make love and art

and become what we created
swim in music we made

but the thing about love,
it's not always there to stay

at least transitory love
love that's a stone for stepping

and landing somewhere
new, with guarded edges

broken vases and plates
kintsugi, the gold glue spilling from within

when one becomes two and what's left
remembers

I was only ever one
anyway

## Peripheral

picket fence
enclosing but in a just-for-looks kinda way
function a lost practicality
pictures a half-inch crooked
plants in need of watering or sun
or something other than me
you in need of something other than me
running circles round my brain
I want to know what it means
to carry less
than the loaded books and rocks
still locked on my back
but carrying less seems to scare me
as if carrying less meant losing more
or worse yet, forgetting
and forgetting is a bottomless loss
of identity, reality, and at long last
existence for the sake of just existing
and am I just existing
if you've already forgotten me?

## How I Spell Love

I like to leave quiet little *I love you's*
subtle things
like buying you something
without saying anything

I won't use it
but if you choose to stay
it will be here for you

leaving notes on nightstands for the next morning
waking and thinking *I miss you even more today*
cleaning the room in my head where my visions of you stay
collecting photos and writings for looking back on one day

saying *you deserve better*
even when better is not the promise I can make

love that knows
truly, I wish nothing but the best for you

and only you know the sculpted edges of the future
you desire

and it is yours to hold and carve out
with or without me

**I Love**

myself – how strange –
I didn't know
my own beauty, gently
when I cry
when I speak
when I smile
I'm expressive
I can be anything
the world is my oyster
I can have anything
whatever I want
is mine
I need not worry
– *stop worrying* –
and when I doubt
remember
how my dad once saw me
because it's time
for me
to be at peace
with me

*Maybe the world isn't for fixing, maybe it's just for accepting. Learning to accept ourselves, learning to accept others, learning to accept the challenges we face.*

## The Star

in the vast
nearly-empty
space
twinkling light
fusing as she orbits
admired and inspiring
a guide
weeping star dust
as years subside
and the stars she draws
nearer to her
far and farther away
a timeless beacon
hope
reminiscent of
bursting
inner light
brightening
the darkest day
and the darkest night

**Rainbow**

at the corners of a sun shower
the rain catches colors –

tears at the corners of eyes
and upturned lips

smiling brightly
in the middle of summer

something of that golden love lingers
and a new love

like kisses of summer rain
and yellow petals pulling toward the sky

reaching, brimming
the likes of joy

beaming as the storms have passed
opening the door to light

and the love that inevitably

lives around you and through you
for now and all eternity

## Acknowledgements

There are more people to thank than pages in this book. For that, Acknowledgements is harder for me to write than the actual poems themselves, but I will attempt to do so while reminding those reading this that even though I may not know you intimately or well, you are part of this book, and I'm thankful you've made it here! Thank you for your support.

I have several professors from UT Austin who inspired, encouraged, and taught me, giving me the courage and skills to publish this book. Most notably of those professors is Laurie Saurborn who read my original thesis *Sun Showers and Moon Flowers*. Without her, the Creative Writing Program, and my kind and thoughtful classmates, many of these poems wouldn't exist today. Additionally, the late Dean Young was my creative writing professor the semester my Dad passed. Although Professor Young has since passed, many of his lessons and words follow me when I write poems to this day.

My chosen family is always top of mind when I think about who I'm grateful for: Taylor Sanders, Tori Aloof, Alyssa

Garza, and Alyssa Rodriguez are a few of my friends who have shown up for me when completing this book (ie being an early reader, offering encouraging words and support all the way). Thank y'all!

Of course I have my blood family to thank, especially my mom for always supporting my endeavors, reading my book, sharing suggestions, and helping me commemorate my dad, no matter how hard it was to relive some of those memories. My dad for insisting that I pursue my passion for writing in college and for being a guiding light for me even after passing. My grandma and papa for giving my imagination space to run wild, for being in my corner, and for my papa who would pick me up on Thursdays after school and ask me what new words I'd learned. His favorite of those being "crochety" and "curmudgeon." My cousin Roxann and her husband, Chris, for being there for me in college, supporting my poetry, and feeding me homemade, gluten-free meals while chatting for hours about stimulating and inspiring topics.

There are a couple of notable grief counselors and therapists that I've had that I'd like to thank. Without whom, I would not feel confident enough to share my voice with the world.

Last, but certainly not least is my remote creative writing group and especially Meg and Fern for offering to be early readers. Thanks to this group, I felt more inspired and encouraged in my endeavors with this book!

## About the Author

Raquel Medora is a Texas native. She received a BA in English from UT Austin with a Creative Writing Certificate in Poetry. Her publications include her first full-length book of poetry, *Moms Are The Strongest Men* (2024). She also published "Fireflies for Eyes" (2017) and "Gerber Daisy" (2019) in Texas' Best Emerging Poets Series. Her poem "I'm Beginning to Think There's No Such Thing as Extroverts" placed first in Pflugerville's annual Poetry Writing Contest (2021). Outside of writing, Raquel is an avid gardener, pulling weeds in her rose-rage garden, planting new seeds and trees, and she enjoys hiking, spending time with her two kids, and enjoying life with her friends.

To see what Raquel is working on next follow her on Instagram **@raquel.medora** or visit her website **https://raquelmedorapoetry.com/**

For submitting a donation to The Glioblastoma Research Organization, please visit Bradley Jay's page:

*I wouldn't want to be here if I didn't believe in the magic of this world and I think it's quite magical you are here.*

*Thank you for being here.*

## The Goodnight Song

Goodnight,
*sleep tight,*

don't let
*the bed bugs bite,*

see you later
*alligator,*

after while
*crocodile,*

goodnight I love you,
*I love you too.*

Goodnight I love you, Dad.

www.ingramcontent.com/pod-product-compliance
Ingram Content Group UK Ltd.
Pitfield, Milton Keynes, MK11 3LW, UK
UKHW012252290726
14090UKWH00016B/606

9 798218 887841